MW00620068

FACETIME WITH GOD

CARLA T. NORTON

Edited by Elaine Sanford

Copyright 2022

All rights reserved.

Scripture quotations noted KJV are from the King James Version of the Holy Bible.

Scripture quotations taken from The Holy Bible, New International Version® NIV® Copyright © 1973 1978 1984 2011 by Biblica, Inc. ™ Used by permission. All rights reserved worldwide.

ACKNOWLEDGEMENT

Special thanks to my wonderful family who are and will always be my greatest supporters. You have been very gracious with allowing me to steal time to frame what began as a prayer. I love the liberty that you have given me to express my ministry in a unique fashion.

Thank you, Rev. Dr. Sister-friend Elaine Sanford who softened the rough edges into palatable morsels fit for the heart and spirit. You have truly been accommodating in gifting your time and energy. May the Lord return the blessing.

Finally, a huge debt of appreciation goes to two women in my Life Group who encouraged me to write: Judith (Last Name) and Rosalind (Last Name). Talk about Holy Ghost bullies, these women were relentless with encouragement, patience, and support. It took several intermissions to convince me, but they only stirred something that was simmering just below the surface.

My prayer is that *Facetime With God* will bless you and stir your spirit.

Genesis: Wake Up!

"Then Jacob awoke from his sleep and said, "Surely the Lord is in this place, and I did not know it."

Jacob had left the home of his parents after deceiving his father and tricking his brother Esau. It had to be a lonely journey as he fled to his uncle's house, hoping to take refuge until the conflict with his brother had blown over. Jacob had grown tired and stopped to rest underneath a tree. As he slept, God revealed to Jacob that just as he had been with his grandfather and father (Abraham and Isaac), God would also be with him. God assured Jacob that the Promise He made to Abraham and then to Isaac, would now be passed along and fulfilled through Jacob. So, although Jacob was feeling lonely, he had never been alone. When Jacob awakened with the reality that God was with him, it gave him encouragement for the future and hope that despite his mistakes and his deceiving others, God was still with him.

PRAYER: Dear God, sometimes as we journey through life, we forget to be still and to hear the plans that you have for our lives. Awaken us from our slumber to new energy and faith to follow the purpose and the path that you have already ordained for us. May we become more sensitive to the moving of Your Spirit – and able to discern that You are leading us – that surely the *Lord is in this place.*

[Genesis (28:16 ESV]

Exodus: I AM

"And God said to Moses, 'I AM WHO I AM'."

In the story of Moses in Exodus chapter 3, God appears as a divine theophany, a flame burning inside a bush that will not be consumed. This manifestation of God was intended to get Moses's attention and to affirm to him that he was being called by God to deliver God's people from bondage in Egypt. Moses was chosen as an ambassador of God for the express purpose of telling the Pharaoh that God said to, "Let my people go". Moses was reluctant to return to Egypt since he had fled the country after killing an Egyptian soldier. But God assured Moses that this call was not a request. God intended for Moses to act as God's emissary and to deliver God's message to Pharaoh. Fearing that he had no authority with Pharaoh nor the ability to persuade the Hebrew people, Moses asked God, *"If I go to the people of Israel and tell them that the God of your ancestors has sent me to you, what will I tell them when they ask, what is his name?* God said to Moses, "tell them that I AM has sent you".

There are so many things that vie for our attention today, and this makes it difficult to discern when God may be trying to get our attention. God may not appear in the form of a divine epiphany, but God may appear in ways that cause us to stop what we are doing and pay attention to HIm. After God has gotten our attention, we too might ask the question: 'Who is asking me to go for Him?'. Well, God may answer, I AM – the one sending you. I AM - what you have been searching for. I AM - your greatest need. I AM - the Truth that you seek. I AM your Life, your strength, and your salvation. Whatever you need, God answers, I AM.

PRAYER: Sovereign God, amid the busyness of our lives, I thank you that you are still showing up in ways that get our attention. Though we may be reluctant to answer your call, we ask that you continue to direct our paths so that we may do the work that you are calling us to do. And, when others ask, by what authority we do this? Help us to answer as Moses did: "I AM has sent me".

[Exodus 3:14a NIV]

Leviticus: Walk With Me

And I will walk among you and will be your God and ye shall be my people.

Leviticus chapter 26 echoes a familiar theme that is found throughout the Holy Scriptures. If you obey the will of God and keep God's commands, then your life will be blessed. Conversely, if you choose to rebel against God, to disobey God's will and commands, then you may miss out on God's blessings and promises that were tailored for you.   As the children of Israel were becoming re-acquainted with the God of Abraham, Isaac, and Jacob, they learned that God expected them to obey the covenant that God had made with their forefathers. If they obeyed the covenant, the people would be blessed. But, if they chose to turn away from it and go their own way, the people would not be blessed; and indeed, would be cursed (Deuteronomy 28). This simple Truth remains true.

Even today, God is still saying, *If you obey me and keep my commands, then I will walk among you. You will be my people and I will be your God.* God has kept this promise. Jesus is the Word of God who "walked among us" and now lives in the heart of every believer. To have this privilege, all you need to do is accept Jesus as your Savior. What a privilege!

PRAYER: Thank you Lord, for walking with me and for making me your treasure. I feel the warmth of your love, your peace, and your presence in my life. You make the difference. That's why I can impact the world!

[Leviticus 26:12]

Numbers: No Limit, No Doubt

The Lord answered Moses, 'Is the Lord's arm too short?
Now you will see whether or not what I say will come true for you'.

On more than one occasion, Moses found himself doubting the power of God. This is surprising since Moses had just seen the power that God displayed when God delivered the children of Israel out of bondage in Egypt. Moses had also seen the power of God on display when God parted the Red Sea and caused God's people to walk through it on dry land. But Pharaoh's army had drowned in the sea. Yet, Moses still doubted the power of God.

It appears that Moses still had much to learn about the God of Abraham, Isaac, and Jacob. He did not understand that there is no limit to what God can do. God asked Moses, "*Is the Lord's arm too short?*" In other words: 'Is God limited in what God can do?'

Beloved, there are times when we doubt the Word of God. If God says it, His Word is always true. God is concerned about every aspect of our lives. So, when we talk to God about our problems or concerns, we should never doubt the power of God to do what we have asked. The writer of I John 5:14 said, *"And this is the confidence that we have in Him, that if we ask anything according to His will, He hears us. And if we know that he hears us, then He shall give us the desires of our heart."* Therefore, even if you think that your concerns such as diet, exercise, or weight control may not be important; if these matters are important to you, then they are also important to God. Talk to him about it – and believe.

[Numbers 11:23 NIV]

Deuteronomy: Blessings

All these blessings will come upon you and accompany you if you obey the Lord your God.

The Old Testament book name Deuteronomy means, "second law or repeated law". It is the fifth book of the Torah. The author, Moses repeats and reminds the Isrealites of the covenant that God made to them. He warns them that disobedience and straying from the laws would only lead to disaster. Keeping the law and commandments would lead to blessings.

In the New Testament, Jesus sums up all the law and commandments by replying,

Love the Lord your God with all your heart, with all your soul and with all your mind. This is the greatest commandment. And the second is like it; Love your neighbor as yourself. All the Law and Prophets hang on these two commandments. Mtt 22:36-40 NIV

PRAYER: Our Father, You promised blessings in every aspect of my life just for obedience. You are always making provisions for my family, my work, my home, and even my finances. You will cause me to prosper. I make you my delight. So, open my eyes to a fresh look at your word. May the fire of your spirit ignite in me an appetite for your word. Nourish my mind and establish and motivate my heart. Strengthen me to do your will as facetime with You. Amen.

[Deuteronomy 28:2 NIV]

Joshua: Be Strong

Have I not commanded you? Be strong and courageous. Do not be terrified; do not be discouraged, for the Lord your God will be with you wherever you go (1:9).

Joshua had matriculated from apprenticeship to leadership. Now it was his time to carry on and to lead God's people into the Promise Land. His mentor was gone. God promised faithfulness. All Joshua needed to do now was to accept his role, step into his strength, and to move forward.

I can remember times when I was on my own and had to be strong and move forward. I attended a university 1600 miles away from home. I took on a leadership role in employment and in ministry. I became a wife, mother, and mentor to my children and family. These were times when someone or something might have been entrusted to my care, and I knew that I had to depend on the Lord. For some, you might need to find your strength to overcome a particularly challenging day at work, at home, or even in your own mind to overcome feelings of depression, alienation, loneliness, or abandonment. Someone may need to find strength to battle addiction, unhealthy habits, or harmful relationships.

It is important to remember that God's faithfulness is the starting point that you need to achieve and/or to overcome the challenges that you face. Joshua was able to do it. I have been able to do it. So, can you. Facetime with God.

Dear Lord, I acknowledge that some things are very frightening and appear insurmountable. You have placed me in charge and have promised Your faithfulness. Remind me that Your faithfulness brings unlimited peace, presence, and power. Your faithfulness brings love, grace, and new mercies. I take courage in knowing that You are my strength. I am equipped for the day! In Christ name, Amen.

[Joshua 1:9 NIV]

Judges: Questions and Answers

And the angel of the Lord appeared unto him and said, "The Lord be with thee, thou mighty man of valor." And Gideon said to him, "Oh my Lord, if the Lord be with us, why then has all this befallen us? And where are all the miracles which our fathers told us, saying, did not the Lord bring us up from Egypt...

Has there been a time in your life when you questioned whether the Lord was with you? Perhaps, you have wondered during the Covid-19 pandemic: Why is this happening to us? Why are so many people dying? Where are the miracles from God? Why doesn't God step in to bring us relief from this terrible scourge? Many people today have more questions about the presence of God than ever before. And no one seems to be bringing forth answers that have any meaning.

Similarly, in the days of the Judges, the children of Israel had rebelled against God and were suffering the consequences of their sin. Gideon had been visited by an angel who told him that though the people were suffering, all was not lost. God had chosen Gideon to step up. All he had to do was to become their leader and tell them what the Lord said. But Gideon was afraid and had been disheartened by what he saw happening to his people. Gideon didn't know what to do. And yet, the angel of the Lord patiently assured Gideon that despite his doubt, the Lord was with him. "I will be with you, have I not sent you?"

Take heart. Facetime with God. Gideon had serious doubt. But God still worked wonders through him. We may have serious doubts. But God will prove God's self for God's Own namesake. The Lord is with you. And, He will do mighty acts through you!

[Judges *6:12-13 NIV*]

Ruth: Faith and Kindness

The Lord repay you for your kindness, and may your reward be full from the LORD, the God of Israel, under whose wings you have come to take refuge!

The story of Ruth may appear to be out-of-place in the Bible, because it is the story of a Moabite woman (a stranger in Israel) who married a wealthy Israelite man and came to be honored by the Israelite people. The faithfulness and kindness that Ruth showed to her mother-in-law Naomi was seen and noted by the people. Ruth also showed her commitment to the God of Israel and this was also impressive to those who saw her. The story of Ruth teaches us several lessons: 1) that God is the God of all people; 2) that God hears and answers the prayers of all who call on His name; 3) that God is faithful and rewards faithfulness; 4) that when kindness is extended, it never goes unnoticed by God; 5) and, finally, that God rewards those who diligently seek him (Hebrews 11:6).

God blessed Ruth, the Moabite woman, while she was working in the fields and then turned the tables and gave Ruth ownership of the field in which she worked. Not only did God bless her in the field, but God elevated her to royalty when she became the grandmother of King David. God gave Ruth (an outsider) full privileges of the inside!

Be faithful, be kind, be committed. Facetime with God-Oh Yes!

[Ruth 2:12 AMP]

13

I Samuel: Praying for Our Children

"For this child I prayed, and the Lord has granted me my petition that I made to Him. Therefore, I have lent him to the Lord. As long as he lives, he is lent to the Lord" (1:27-28).

In the opening of this book, we find a woman barren, unable to have children but still praying and requesting of the Lord that she has a child (son). We find Hannah was in a good place with a husband who was good to her. He furnished Hannah with all she needed but yet, she was empty. On the outside, we have judged others that seemingly have everything they want and yet, there is a space that only God can fill. God granted Hannah's request.

Parents take a cue from Hannah. Pray for your children even before you have them. Hannah returned the child back to the Lord by dedicating his life to the Lord. We can do similarly by praying for our children and by teaching them to love the Lord.

It is important that they are surrounded by godly influence. In a time of social distancing, remember the God is not distanced. Remind your children that God loves them and loves to hear their voices. God will turn his face toward them. All we need do is turn our hearts and face to Him.

Dear God, we pray for our children. Watch over them and give them hearts that will seek after you. We pray for their peers. Give our children discerning hearts and surround them with godly influence. Keep them strong in body, mind, and spirit. Protect their creativity and innovative minds and allow them to maintain the ability to laugh. Thank you for the gift of children. We give them back to You. In the name of our Christ, Amen.

II Samuel: Sitting Before the Lord

"And now, O Lord God, You are God and your words are true, and you have promised this good thing to your servant (7:28)."

King David had a desire to build a house for the Lord after the Lord had given him rest from all his enemies. Nathan the prophet replied, "do all that is in your heart for God is with you." But the Lord had a better plan for David and sent Nathan with a word and a surer promise. God told David that one of his sons would build a house, but more importantly, God would establish his everlasting covenant with David. That promise is that a throne and a kingdom will come from the lineage of David. And this kingdom will have no end.

David facetimed God. He sat before the Lord after Nathan had brought him the news. David worshipped the Lord. After you have heard, read, or received a word from the Lord, try sitting before the Lord and worship. Perhaps you say, I have not heard a word from the Lord. Try this. Breathe in, hold it for three seconds, then exhale. Let everything that has breath, praise the Lord. God desires to bless you and your family and will establish His covenant with you. This is the word of the God for the people of God.

I Kings: The Right Choice

"And Elijah came unto all the people and said, "How long halt you between two opinions? If the Lord be God, follow him (18:21)."

Elijah the prophet of God challenged the four hundred and fifty prophets of Baal to a showdown to prove who was the true God. Elijah called the people together and asked them to choose. No need of vacillating back and forth.

Today, we must also choose. There is no need of straddling the fence. If God is God, choose God. How often we are blinded by our own pride, lust of the eye, and the cares of life. We go after things with unrelenting determination. If only we would go after God with such vigor and persistence. We will find God when we turn our face to Him and seek Him with all of our whole heart.

God answered Elijah with consuming fire. God was not away on a journey, or talking to someone else, nor asleep. God is 'woke'. When we face time with God, we have His undivided attention as if we are the only one. The Lord is God and only God can do that.

Father, we choose you. Amen

II Kings: Open Our Eyes

"And when the servant got up and went out early the next day, an army with horses and chariots had surrounded the city. "Oh my lord, what shall we do?" the servant asked. "Don't be afraid," the prophet answered. "Those who are with us are more than those who are with them." And Elisha prayed, "O Lord, open his eyes so he may see." Then the Lord opened the servant's eye, and he looked and saw the hills full of horses and chariots of fire all around Elisha (6:15-18 NIV).

Have you ever awakened and before you began your day, trouble after trouble seems to block or hinder your progress, your peace, and your purpose for the day? Often, we see the myriad of challenges. We are in a pandemic and even now we count our stresses before we see the blessing. Someone said that our troubles are opportunities-or present opportunities for miracles and blessings. You are up for the challenge.

Stand firm. Elisha prayed that the Lord would open his servant's eyes to see the vast army of the Lord surrounding them, armed and ready to do battle on their behalf.

Dear God, open our eyes that we may see You. Just in case, we cannot see the answer, teach us to close our eyes, and walk by faith. The power of God is mighty to save. We are surrounded by a great cloud of witness. If God is for us, who, or what can be against us? If God is for us, it is more than the world, more than the pandemic, more than visible or invisible trouble or problems that are against us. Jesus Christ who transcends time

18

and space, is the same yesterday (Old Testament), today (presently) and forever more (eternity).

I Chronicles: It's a Heart Thing

"Give thanks unto the Lord, call upon His name, make known his deeds among his people. Sing to Him. Tell of all His wonderous works. Glory in His holy name. Let the heart of those who seek the Lord rejoice...Look to the Lord and His strength, seek his face continually (16:8,11)

King David had returned the ark of the covenant in its rightful place and sacrificed before the Lord. He began to offer this psalm to instruct the Levites (the priesthood) and the people to give praise to the Lord in this manner.

Today, we do not have a physical "ark" placed in a tent or temple, but we do have a covenant. The rightful place of that covenant is in our hearts. The covenant is more than legalism - head knowledge. It is a matter of the heart. Our sacrifice is a sacrifice of praise. Give thanks to the Lord and let your heart be glad. Seek his face. Do not seek only his hand. God is indeed the gift giver, but so much more than the gifts that He gives us. Look to the Lord. Facetime God. I dare you to see Him for yourself. You will begin to praise as David and proclaim God's goodness and God's strength. There is discovery in praise. I am still discovering as I facetime with God. You will too.

II Chronicles: Heal Our Land

"If my people, which are called by my name, shall humble themselves and pray, and seek my face and turn from their wicked ways, then will I hear from heaven and will forgive their sin and will heal their land (7:14).

King Solomon finished building the temple and dedicated it to the Lord. He offered praise to God and prayer. This is the answer to Solomon from the Lord.

God's response to Solomon is also God's response to us today. We are his people called by His name. More than ever, we need to humble ourselves. Pride is rampant, as is wickedness in high places, and low places. Let us return to God.

Forgive us Lord and heal us. Heal our land. It is Your promise to us.

"O God, will you not judge them, for we have no power to face this vast army that is attacking us. We do not know what to do but our eyes are upon you." And the Lord answered, "This is what the Lord says to you. Be not afraid nor be discouraged because of this vast army, for the battle is not yours, but God'. You will not have to fight this battle. Take up your positions; stand firm and see the deliverance the Lord will give you... (20:12, vs. 15, vs. 17)."

This world is rapidly changing before our very eyes. This year alone, has presented unimaginable challenges that test our moral convictions and the foundation of our faith. Unprecedented times brought on by a pandemic requires us to live differently. It has caused us to do community, school, and church differently.

We are forced to think innovatively on how we celebrate life and challenged by how we honor our dead. Mental health issues are on the rise but before we totally despair, God is saying take your position in me, stand firm and I will deliver because I will fight for you. God **always** wins.

Ezra: Work of the Lord

"And I was strengthened as the hand of the Lord my God was upon me, and I gathered together out of Israel chief men to go up with me (7:28b)

The books of Ezra and Nehemiah show how God is able to take their passion, a desire of the heart, a dream to rebuild the temple (which lay in ruins in Jerusalem) and bring it to fruition; God gave the people of God, the remnant community a heart to join in the work. Many are named, but more importantly it is the willingness of the people to obey God and rebuild. God caused King Cyrus and King Darius, non-Jewish kings to help finance, furnish, and authorize this rebuilding with protection from others (nations) who would have fought against it.

Have you ever had a dream or passion to achieve a goal, but it looked like there were no resources, or your resources lay in ruin? Or perhaps you thought that your dream could not be attained because you felt that you were unskilled, incapable of carrying it out or just too old or you knew that this dream was too big for you alone? Like Ezra, there were some who came against his dream and wanted to deter, discourage, or kill his dream. There may be some telling you that you can't do this. But there are others who say, "We can do this!"

Know for certain that when you are doing the work of the Lord, there will be adversity that wants to stop, hinder, stunt your growth, discourage your mind and/or distract your purpose, but, continue the work. The Lord will strengthen you to fulfill that God-given purpose. If needed, join in a community of faith with like-minded supporters to lighten the load. Turn your face to Him. God is able to assign assistance to you from places you would have never thought. I am learning that God will provide scaffolding if needed then remove it when not needed. God does not want us to become dependent on the scaffolding, but dependent on Him.

"Two are better than one, because they have a good return for their labor. For they can help each other to succeed" (Eccl 4:9-12 NIV).

By all means, pray and watch God cause your dream to become a reality. You must do like Ezra and **do** the work. So, what are you waiting for? Take courage. Now that you have prayed about it, trust God. Focus and plan it. When adversity arrives, praise God knowing that you MUST be on to something Big! The hand of the Lord is upon you. Strengthen your resolve and you will find that there are others who will cheer you on and help you move forward. Enjoy the journey!

Nehemiah: Hand of the Lord

"Then I told them of the hand of my God which was good upon me... And they said, let us rise up and build. So they strengthened their hands for this good work. Nehemiah said, ... This day is holy to our Lord. Do not grieve, for the joy of the Lord is your strength" (2:18).

The people who had returned from exile to Jerusalem rebuilt the walls of Jerusalem and the temple. Although it was not easy, they persevered and accomplished the task because the "good hand of the Lord" was upon them. Nehemiah and Ezra the scribe led the charge. As with Ezra, the adversary wanted to frustrate the work, intimidate the workers, and tried to hold power over and maintain systemic racism over the Jews. The Jews took steps to ensure that the work was done by identifying the enemies' tactics; preparing for battle as they armed themselves; and keeping their eyes on God and their focused goal.

God often gives us a task that we are able to accomplish, not because of our own abilities, but by the good hand of the Lord on our lives. Many times, opportunities are disguised as obstacles, but there are times if we do not persevere, obstacles very much like systemic racism, power privilege and discouragement can hinder our progress. When the work was done, Nehemiah encouraged the people not to weep but to be joyous. This was a time to rejoice. This was the time to praise God for His goodness. Often, we forget to be glad for the things that God has done. When we look back, we are strengthened that God did it before, He certainly can and will do it again

Esther: Elevation

Do not think that because you are in the king's house, you alone of all the Jews will escape. For if you remain silent at this time, relief and deliverance for the Jews will arise from another place, but you and your father's house will perish. And who knows but that you have come to your royal position for such a time as this?

I can think of no other book of the bible where timing was more important than God's timing in the book of Esther. The Lord elevated a young Jewish girl from poverty and captivity in a foreign land to a position of power as queen. The book of Esther is one of two books of the bible that is named for a woman whom God elevates from rags to riches. The second woman was Ruth; and it cannot be a coincidence that Esther was a Jew who married a non-Jew, while Ruth was a non-Jew who married a Jew. Surely, we learn that despite the racism that may exist in our society, the Lord is no respecter of persons. The book of Esther is a classic example of this as it tells the story of one man's failed plot to destroy the entire nation of Jewish people. The plan had been set in motion simply because of hate and animosity. But God's divine hand intervened and caused a young woman from the hated race to become favored above all other maidens in the land. And, Esther was not only chosen by the king to sit as his side, but she became queen over all of the people including the evil man who was trying to destroy her people. God's plan always exceeds human plans. Esther's position of power enabled her to save the Jewish nation of people and to save herself.

The story of Esther should suggest to us that we must not assume that we are immune from unjust treatment just because we are in a certain socio-economic bracket. It could be that the Lord has elevated you to a status of prosperity and influence "for such a time as this." Perhaps, you have successfully climbed the corporate ladder and are sitting comfortably in a role of leadership. Could your voice be the voice that is needed to bring attention to the hurt, harm or injustice that surrounds you? Facetime with God and find your answer.

PRAYER: Heavenly Father, thank you for the opportunity to make a difference and to influence the world for good. May truth be a guiding principle as your Spirit leads me to do as Esther did and speak for those who are unable to speak for themselves. In Christ name, Amen.

[Esther 4:13-14 KJV]

Job: Difficult Circumstances

Will the one who contends with the Almighty correct him?
Let him who accuses God answer him (40:2. Furthermore, God
asks Job, "Where were you when I laid the foundations of the
earth? Tell me if you understand. Who marked off its dimensions?
Surely you know! (38:5)

Job is the Bible character that is best recognized for having patience. Have you heard the reference: the patience of Job? Through one tragic episode after another, Job had suffered grief and loss, and yet he remained faithful to God. Even after his wife had urged Job to turn away from God, Job did not listen and maintained his integrity. Job said to her, "Shall we accept good from the Lord and not trouble?" (2:10). But Job's patience had apparently worn thin over time and caused him to demand that God explain why such tragedy had happened to him. Job, a mere man, challenged the Almighty God, and He answered Job. But God did the demanding (40:2).

It is perfectly acceptable to ask God to give us the wisdom to understand the difficult circumstances that we encounter in our lives. But God may not be called upon to explain why God permits some things to happen. God is Sovereign which means that God does not answer to us. God takes counsel only from God's Own Himself. "Who has known the mind of the Lord and who has been his counselor? (Romans 11:34). This was an important lesson that Job had to learn.

The gospel writer affirms in Matthew 5:45 that, "He [the Lord] makes his sun to rise on the evil and on the good and sends rain on the just and on the unjust." Many people ask the question: why do bad things happen to good people? The answer according to Scripture is that: Bad things can happen to good people, just as good things can happen to bad people. This is simply a fact that we must all face as part of the human condition. Job failed to realize that God does not owe us an explanation. This is a hard lesson for many of us to receive.

Job had suffered the pain of losing his children and all that he possessed. He was grieving which was a normal process for him to experience. But, we must know that as we grieve, God knows, understands and feels the anguish that we are enduring. God consoles broken hearts. Facetime with God. Wait in patience for Him. Amen.

[Job 38:5, 40:2 NIV]

Psalms: Seek My Face

"When you said, seek my face, my heart said to you, Your face Lord, will I seek

Through 150 different Psalms, we are invited to enter into communion with a Holy God through songs, prayers, lamentations, meditations and even through the ministry of silence as we reverence and praise Our Lord. The people of ancient days have given us a model to follow as we come into the presence of God Our Father where we may lay out our pain, our anguish, our anger, our sadness and sorrow, and our victories. The psalms enable us to express the emotions of our inner most being. They capture the expressions that we are not able to put into words. When one is depressed, just read from the psalms and before long, contentment enters your spirit and joy will enter your heart. You said, "Seek my face. And, I responded, "Your face will I seek."

What is your reaction as you read from the psalms? Your heart is answering the calling of the Lord to "Seek my face." Facetime with God! Seek His face. Sit in His Presence and be confident that as you seek His face, God will reward you with goodness and blessings in every facet of life. In His presence is sufficiency, grace, glory, and joy. Today, in the 21st Century, we can still seek His face. We can Facetime with God.

[Psalm 27:8 NIV]

Proverbs: Trust God

Trust in the Lord with all your heart and lean not on your own understanding. In all your ways acknowledge Him, and He will direct your path.

The Proverbs are filled with so many wonderful words of instructions, encouragement, and wisdom. They are a collection of wise sayings designed to help those who trust God to lead a wise and meaningful life. My mother often read them to me as a child, even this particular proverb which calls upon believers to trust in the Lord. We can trust the Lord because He has proven that He is trustworthy. To trust God means to: rely, lean, depend, and *release your heart* to the safe-keeping of the Lord. We can always trust God who is the Father of wisdom, understanding and knowledge. As a matter of fact, He is God who will *perfect that which concerns us and will bring it to completion.* Facetime with God and learn to trust Him.

Proverbs 3:5-6

The wisdom of the proverbs is often reflected in short, pithy statements that carry a profound meaning such as: *A merry heart does good like a medicine ...*

Laughter is good for the mind, body, and the spirit. Have you had a good dose of laughter lately? Can you even recall the last time that you laughed out loud? One of the most beautiful sounds to me is to hear the laughter of children. It tickles the funny bone just hearing their light-hearted cackles. Scientists and health professionals often agree that laughter releases endorphins in the body that help us with healing and relaxation. So, get a good dose of laughter today as you consider this: The God who created a duckbill platypus must have had a sense of humor. If you don't think that is funny, take a look in the mirror and smile. Turn those frowns upside down and laugh! *For the joy of the Lord is your strength.*

[Proverbs 17:22 NIV]

Ecclesiastes: Fear God

"Let us hear the conclusion of the whole matter, fear God and keep His commandments. For this is the whole duty of man. (12:13-14).

What would you do if you had more wisdom than anyone else – and you had more money than you could ever spend? This is what happened to the third king of Israel, King Solomon, whom God blessed to be the wisest man who ever lived. Solomon asked God for wisdom to lead God's people. This request pleased the Lord and God decided to bless him with abundant wisdom, wealth, and everything else that Solomon could desire. But God had cautioned Solomon that with wisdom and power also comes responsibility. He warned Solomon to keep his focus on God, to obey God's commands and to not be lured away by the visible pleasures of the world.

But Solomon could not resist over-indulging himself from food and drink to wine and women – he took whatever his heart desired and forgot about the warnings from God. He could not resist the temptation to fulfill his every desire. And after he had done it all, his mind finally told him what his heart had tried to reveal: *"... the conclusion of the matter is to fear God and keep His commands. For this is the whole duty of man."* If one does not do this, then nothing else that he does will truly satisfy.

Dear God, I pray for an understanding heart that I may be true to You, myself and to others. Help me to discern good from evil that I may always walk justly before you. May You become my treasure over any other desire. Help me to avoid being blinded by today's *bling*. And in every season of my life, let me be found *chasing after you*.

[Ecclesiastes 12:13-14 NIV]

Song of Solomon: My Banner

He brought me to his banqueting table, His banner over me is love. 2:4).

The Song of Solomon is given as a descriptive love song that reflects the longing and desires of a young man for a Shunamite woman, his bride to be. She expresses her love and deep desire for him. And, he likewise, expresses his longing and desire for her. The book is intended as an allegorical reference of God's personal and intimate relationship with God's people. It is further intended to reflect Israel's desire and love for God though we know that her love often wavered from God.

As the reader engages the text, he or she should imagine the depth of love that God has for Gods people even when we fail Him. How can one define the intricate feelings that God has for us? How can love be poured out in words that express the tender love of God?

As a child during summer Vacation Bible School, I learned a song that, *God is Jehovah-Nissi* meaning that *the Lord is my Banner*. This brought me comfort back then and it still brings me comfort today to know the depth of love that God has for me. He looks on me with affection, with compassion and with great caring. He prepares a table before me filled with choice blessings beyond what I can imagine. His love is unrivaled, and I delight in His good pleasure. He gives me the desires of my heart and His banner covers me. His banner covers you. His banner over me is love. Facetime with the God of Love.

[Song of Solomon 2:4 NIV; www.names.org].

Isaiah: God With Us

Therefore, the Lord himself will give a sign; Behold, a virgin shall conceive, and bear a son, and shall call his name Immanuel (7:14).

Over 400 years before the physical birth of Jesus into the world, the Prophet Isaiah foretold his coming. Through the Spirit of the Lord, he prophesied that the one born of a virgin would be called *Immanuel or God with us*. It was not the prediction of just another birth. But it was the sign that the long-awaited Messiah would be born of a virgin and would be the very Son of God. God the Father would send God's own son, clothed in human form, born into an uncaring world. He would live among us as *fully man and fully God*. The writer Eugene Peterson said, "He moved into the neighborhood."

The story of Jesus's coming into the world is amazing and awe-inspiring no matter how many times you hear it. The Savior of the world was born as a common man and endured the same emotions as that of common men. He felt joy and love, betrayal and grief. He had friends and frenemies - Haters and enemies. *"We do not have a High Priest who cannot sympathize with our weaknesses; but we have [a High Priest] who has been tempted in every way as we are, and yet He did not sin (Hebrews 4:15)."*

Jesus was and remains "God with Us", and He understood the great chasm that exists between man and God. That is why He left the riches and glory of Heaven to come into the world so that He could step in as the ultimate sacrifice to save all humanity. "God with Us" set the example for sacrificial love which cost us nothing – but cost Him everything. What a price He paid. Oh, what a great debt we owe to "God with Us"!

[Isaiah 7:14 NIV]

Jeremiah: The Master Plan

Behold, I am the Lord, the God of all flesh; Is there anything too hard for me?

During the time of Israel's captivity at the hands of the Babylonians, Jeremiah was the chief prophet. God told Jeremiah that judgment had been passed on the people and that they would be taken into captivity by their enemies. But God had also told Jeremiah to go out and to buy a field. Well this didn't make much sense to Jeremiah. Why should he buy a field, if the land would be overtaken and the people taken into captivity? It didn't make sense to Jeremiah, but it was all part of God's plan. God had to remind Jeremiah that God has the master plan. Though Jeremiah might not know it. God knows the beginning – and God knows the end. All Jeremiah needed to do was to trust God and believe that it would all turn out for the good. Was it not possible for God to restore what God had allowed to be destroyed? It was an important lesson for Jeremiah to learn.

Has God given you a dream or vision that others are not able to see? What projects, ministries or tasks are you trying to achieve for the Lord, but obstacles seem to stand in your way? It is possible that the passion you feel has come from the Lord who has placed a yearning inside you to achieve His perfect will. It might not make sense to others. In fact, it might not make sense to you. But it could be an indicator that God intends for you to achieve it. Trust God and achieve the impossible.

[Jeremiah 32:27 ESV]

Lamentations: I Have Hope!

This I recall to mind, therefore I have hope. It is of the Lord's mercies that we are not consumed, because his compassions fail not. They are new every morning; great is thy faithfulness.

There is an often-repeated statement: 'it could have been worse'. This typically means that one is not experiencing the ultimate fate that could have been dispensed. The writer implies this status for the people of Israel who had blatantly turned their backs on God and had even had the audacity to worship other gods inside the temple established for the Lord. Judgment had now come upon Israel and they were enduring the chastisement they deserved. But it could have been worse said the writer. As he thought about the tender mercies of the Lord and how good God had been to them over the years, he realized that they deserved total destruction.

It is the same as every sinner must admit to him or herself. The wages of sin is death. We who sin deserve death. But, because we serve a God who loves us, His compassions never fail, and God never ceases to forgive. God is merciful. God is forgiving. It is because of His mercy that we are not utterly consumed.

When you awaken to a new day, you are greeted by the mercies of the Lord. They are fresh every morning, personalized and tailor-made just for you. God is immersed in the situations of your life and He is faithfully working on your behalf. May you walk in peace, confidently knowing that His tender mercies are more than enough. Facetime with God today.

[Lamentations 3:21-22 KJV]

Ezekiel: A New Start

I will give you a new heart and put a new spirit in you, I will remove from you your heart of stone and give you a heart of flesh

The people of Israel were longing for the day when the Lord would deliver them from exile in a foreign land and restore them to the covenant relationship that they once enjoyed with God. Prophets like Ezekiel had foretold that God's anger would not last forever; that God would indeed one day forgive His people and would restore them back to right relationship with Him.

But, a right relationship with Israel would mean starting all over with God. The Lord would give them a new beginning, a new spirit, and a new heart. This meant that they must let go of the stony heart that had caused them to turn away from God and to embrace idolatry and rebellion. And they must be willing to receive a new heart and spirit which would mark their new beginning.

The Lord God gives us a new heart that beats in rhythm with His Own. May we willingly receive a heart of love and turn away the heart of stone. The heart of the matter is that we are God's greatest treasure. The warmth of God's love melts our ice-cold hearts such that we may see ourselves in a new light. The light of the Lord enables us to care for God, for others and ourselves.

[Ezekiel *36:26 NIV*]

Daniel:

If it be so, our God whom we serve is able to deliver us from the burning fiery furnace and he will deliver us out of thine hand, O king. But if not, be it known unto thee, O king, that we will not serve thy gods, nor worship the golden image that thou hast set up

Someone once said that, *if you don't stand up for something, you will fall for anything.* The story of the three Hebrew boys is found in the prophetic book of Daniel. During the reign of King Nebuchadnezzar of Babylon, the three young men had been among the many captives taken from their land of Judah and brought into exile in Babylon. The people there had strange customs and mannerisms which included the worshipping of idol gods. So, these young men got into trouble right away when they openly defied the king by refusing to bow down and worship his idol. Apparently, death by fire was not their worst fear as they told the king of their belief in God. In fact, they told him that God would deliver them out of the king's hand. But they added quickly, that even if God chose not to deliver them, they would not dishonor God by bowing to a handmade idol.

Do you have the kind of faith that would enable you to take a stand? Would you have the kind of faith that would embolden you to stand up for God regardless of what it might cost you? Faith often seems strong when things are going well. But, the real test of faith is what we do when the chips are down. It is what we do when there is much to lose.

PRAYER: Father, I pray that I will walk confidently and absolutely assured that no one or nothing can take Your place in my life. I pray that no division or compromise will ever enter my relationship with you. Enable me to walk in Your strength and stand in Your power when the heat is on. I know that the test by the fire will bring me out as pure gold. I worship You.

Daniel 3:17-18

Hosea

For I desired mercy, and not sacrifice; and the knowledge of God more than burnt offerings.

Have you ever loved someone or perhaps cared for them deeply? If so, your heart was probably so tender toward that person that you were willing to overlook many of their faults. Hosea knew what this kind of love was like. He loved a woman dearly, but she gave her love to others. She broke Hosea's heart. And yet, no matter what she did, Hosea was always willing to forgive and accept her back.

Hosea's story is a metaphor for God's love for Israel and for us. Despite the fact that Israel kept turning away from God, God was always forgiving and willing to accept her back. Likewise, in our case today, God forgives and accepts us back because He still desires a sincere relationship with us. God does not want the repetitive and empty praise that we often offer up each Sunday. But He desires true and authentic worship that comes from a repentant heart. The irony is that God needs nothing from us – and we need everything from God. And yet, it is God who continually reaches out seeking to draw us back to Himself. God wants us to know Him. God wants us to be in relationship with Him. Just as Hosea wanted his bride to return to him alone, God wants His bride – the Children of God (the Church) to return to a faithful, loving relationship with Him. God loves us sincerely.

[Hosea 6:6   KJV]

Joel

And everyone who calls on the name of the Lord will be saved.

As a young child, my son had to conquer the fear of the height of the "big slide". There were two slides at the park. One was the 'kiddie slide' which was for the little children, but the other was the big slide-twice as tall. It towered the little slide and just the thought of climbing it was pretty daunting for a four-year-old.

It took courage to climb the ladder of big slide but once up, the imperious height made him cry out for help. As a good parent, I came to the rescue to coax him down while making his seemingly impossible journey; not only a possibility, but convincingly one that he would make repeatedly.

I believe that there is a drive in everyone to push the envelope and reach beyond their normal grasp. I believe it is God-inspired, although sometimes we reach for misguided goals and desperately needed a Savior. Occasionally we may find that we have attained all that we reached for and still found a void that only God can fill. Call. Just as a parent came to the rescue for their child, God comes to our rescue and saves.

Amos

Do two walk together unless they have agreed to do so?
(3:3 NIV)

Little in this life compares to having a good friend whether he or she is a family member, or someone held dear to your heart. A friend tells you NOT what you want to hear but speaks the truth in love even if it might hurt. A friend is someone who can be trusted with your joys, fears, sorrows, and tears. Secrets are safe with friends and within the bounds of friendship even 'bloopers' are not used against you. Laughter is heard and love abounds between friends. Friends help to build character and to encourage dreams with words and actions. Friends are able to walk together because they can agree in spirit though they may not agree in words.

Amos expresses God's disappointment with the nation of Israel which had turned its back on God. God had indeed been Deliverer and friend to Israel, but Israel had not been a faithful friend to their faithful God. The people had chosen injustice and turned away from God's commands. They had nothing in common with the God who had shielded and protected them over the many years of their nation. Israel and the Lord could no longer 'walk together' for they could no longer agree; however, the Lord promised that He would keep his covenant and redeem and restore Israel and they would walk together again.

PRAYER: Dear God, I pray for my friend today. Thank you for letting our paths cross at this time in our lives. Bless them with peace and meet their needs according to your good purpose in their lives. May we draw closer to your heart and to each other. And should we find that our friends are few, we ask you to turn our hearts to You that we may find (as the songwriter said), "What a friend we have in Jesus." Amen.

[Amos 3:3   NIV]

Obadiah

The day of the Lord is near for all nations. As you have done, it will be done to you; your deeds will return upon your own head.

You have heard of the golden rule, "Do *unto others as you will have them do unto you."* We should be aware that throughout the Old and New Testament are echoes of this principle which is referred to as reciprocity. In essence, it means that what you do to others, will be done to you. The seeds you sow will spring up in your own harvest. And the expression that *you reap what you sow* is not just a trite expression but an invaluable truth.

God is a God of Justice. Not only will God judge you, but God, Our Creator also judges nations. *The Lord* will judge us individually. And the Lord will also judge us as a nation collectively. It is important how we treat others, intentionally.

Let us remember to pray for our nation, for our churches, for our government, and especially for our leaders. Pray that the God of All Creation and Justice will have mercy upon us who have failed to obey His commands. *The day of the Lord is near for all nations*.

Sovereign God,

We pray for our nation. Bless our leaders with wisdom and direction as they lead. May they rule justly and righteously with the audacity to be equitable in their dealings out of a true heart and conscious. We pray that that our leaders serve with integrity, innovation, and justly pursuing peace for all.

[Obadiah 1:15 NIV

Jonah

This terrified them and they asked, "What have you done?"
(They knew he was running away from the Lord because he had
already told them so.)

In the beginning of the story of Jonah, we can already tell
that trouble is brewing for the prophet. The text reveals that
Jonah "ran away from the Lord (v.3)." So, it is reasonable to
assume that Jonah is about to be in big trouble! How does he
plan to get away from the Lord? Jonah chose to hide himself
aboard a ship and to sail away to another land. But Jonah forgot
that no ship could hide him from the eyes of God because God
could find Jonah wherever he decided to go. The psalmist asked
the question in Psalm 139:7, "Where can I go to flee from your
spirit?" Jonah had hidden himself aboard a ship, but he awakened
to find the ship embroiled in a raging storm. The sailors were
trying to keep the ship afloat, but nothing that they could do was
working. Clearly the men had experienced storms at sea in the
past. But this storm was unlike any they had known. How could
they save themselves? What could they do? The sailors
determined that this storm was caused by God and Jonah was the
culprit. Jonah gave the only answer. The men would have to
throw Jonah into the sea. The rest is his-story.

This storm happened because Jonah refused to obey God.
Is it possible that some of the storms that we face in life are
because we too have turned a deaf ear to God? Could God be
calling you to take on a task, but you have been reluctant to do

so? Or could He be calling you to use a special gift or talent, but you have persisted in refusing?

Jonah answered the call and finally obeyed. The impact of Jonah's obedience was unimaginable. I myself have finally accepted the call to put pen to paper and begin to write down my thoughts. What task has God called on you to do? Facetime God and get busy before the storm appears!

PRAYER: Dear God, give us strength and confidence for the task that you have set before us. Your way is best. Refresh our faith and renew our trust in You. We know that our obedience will provide encouragement and blessings to others. And that our disobedience can only bring struggle and hardship to ourselves and possibly others.

[Jonah 1:10 NIV]

Micah

He has showed you, O man, what is good. And what does the Lord require of you? To act justly and to love mercy and to walk humbly with your God.

As we look around in our world it is not difficult to see the injustice that affects the lives of many of God's people: from the homeless who cannot afford a place to live to those who battle sickness and disease with little or no access to proper healthcare. Many children are denied a quality education or healthcare while others receive the best that money can buy. The list of unfairness and injustice is longer than any of us can record. The face of injustice is multi-faceted and multi-cultural. It affects all people in all places in all times.

Merriam Webster defines justice as relational, impartial, and fair. One extends justice when one lives in right relationship with God and humanity; ever doing what is right in creation and in our environment. Are you a leader that may be called "just?"

As we facetime God, remember that justice takes the spot-light off of what we do for ourselves and focuses it on what we do for others. The skill of extending justice is sharpened through humility and walking with God and others. This is what the Lord requires. And God says, "It is good."

Dear God,

Help us to walk humbly before You as we facetime You by being kind and merciful to others and to ourselves.

[Micah 6:8 NIV]

Nahum: Our Stronghold

The Lord is good, a refuge in times of trouble. He cares for those who trust in him.

Praise God for He is good. God cares for you and me. In the day of trouble, we have a refuge, a stronghold. In military terms, the stronghold is a fortified place of protection, a garrison, a secured place especially during battles or attacks. In our time of distress or attack, we can run to the Lord and confidently, positively trust Him with assurance.

The name of the Lord is a strong tower. The righteous run into it and are safe. Proverbs 18:10

PRAY: I pray that you will see how valuable you are in the eyes of God. When trouble arises, may you run to the One who runs to you with a mighty army of protection. God is good and is always trustworthy.

[Nahum 1:7 NIV]

Habakkuk: Make It Plain

And the Lord answered me, and said, Write the vision, and make it plain on tablets, so he may run who reads it.

Habakkuk wondered as so many of us today, how those who are wrong seemed to get away with murder? God answered compassionately that the godless nation will be judged. God assures us today, that *the just shall live by faith*. Faith is not just an opinion in what one sees or hears, but it is the conviction that what God says, God will perform no matter how long it takes.

God gives each of us a purpose for our lives. Many of us do not really understand what it is, but we know that it is somehow tied to our passion and our vision. God knows each personality and fits each promise and dream individually.

Face time God. Be still. Hear His voice. The Spirit will guide you into God's plan for your life. Write it down. Journal about it. The vision may become plain, by faith. Then run to achieve it.

[Habakkuk 2:2 NIV]

Zephaniah: A Brighter Day

The Lord thy God (in the midst of thee) is mighty: He will save. He will rejoice over thee with joy. He will rest in his love. He will joy over thee with singing.

The writer of Hebrews 12:6 said, "Whom the Lord loves, He chastens" and this was the case with Israel. The people had been held captive by their enemies for 70 years because they had turned their back on their covenant with God; and had even turned to worshipping idol gods. But, Zephaniah prophesies about a brighter day when the Lord God would forgive, and Israel would once again be restored to fellowship with Him. The Lord was still in their midst and He would save them from total destruction.

May you also recognize the love of God afresh. Regardless of your past faults, you can walk again with your head held high when you come to the reality that (though He might remain silent) God is still with you every second of your life. He awakens you with a gentle song. And, when the day is done, His lullabies calm your inner spirit and bring you to peaceful rest. The Psalmist declares that you will not *fear the terror by night nor the arrows that fly by day* (Psalm 91:5) for He is with you.

Who is the King of glory? The Lord strong and mighty, the Lord mighty in battle (Psalm 24:8). Mighty to save. Facetime with the Ever-Present God.

[Zephaniah 3:17 KJV]

Haggai

The latter glory of this house shall be greater than of the former, says the Lord of hosts. And in this place I will give peace, declares the Lord of hosts.

In the days of the Prophet Haggai, the magnificent temple that Solomon had built for the Lord had been destroyed by Israel's enemies. Efforts to rebuild the edifice had been hampered by their adversaries. And the people were disheartened by the feeling that they could never rebuild the temple such that it would once again be Israel's proudest achievement. But Haggai brought a message from the Lord that the people must not grow weary and they must not mourn over the temple of the past. Instead, God wanted them to keep working and to rebuild this temple. *For I will fill this house with glory, said the Lord Almighty.* (v.7). The temple must be rebuilt!

In this climate of Covid-19, congregations have not been able to gather together as they once did prior to the onset of the virus. Now, more than ever, people are beginning to come to the reality that church (as we once knew it), may not return. Having to 'do church' differently has caused us all to focus on what it really means to worship God. Do we have to go to a certain building in order to commune with God? When Jesus spoke to the woman at the well, He said, *The hour is coming, and now is here, when the true worshiper will worship the Father in spirit and in truth. For the Father is seeking such people to worship him. God is a Spirit, and they that worship him must worship him in spirit and in truth* (John 4:23-24). Though we may be disheartened at the thought of not being able to gather together in a building, we must never forget that God does not dwell in buildings made by human hands. Therefore, we do not need buildings in order to worship Our Lord and Savior who is everywhere at the same time. And, He lives in you and me!

PRAYER: Lord Almighty, we reverence You. And, though our world is driving us to worship through the means of technology, we will not neglect our worship of you. We will continue to devote our lives and our hearts to worshipping you for we realize that though we are distant from each other, You are never socially distanced from us. We thank you for the continued reminder that you do not dwell in buildings, but in our hearts.

[Haggai 2:9 KJV]

Zechariah

Rejoice greatly, O daughter of Zion! Shout aloud, O daughter of Jerusalem! Behold, your King is coming to you; righteous and having salvation is He, humble and mounted on a colt, the foal of a donkey (9:9 ESV).

Hundreds of years before Jesus appeared, the Prophet Zechariah prophesied the good news of the coming of the Messiah as king over God's people. There had been many years of sorrow and sadness following their years in captivity and broken covenant relationship with God. So, news of the coming of a Savior had to bring great joy to the hearts of the people.

Zechariah painted a picture of the Messiah's triumphal entry into Jerusalem – not as a mighty warrior riding on a stallion. But he presents an image of humility and peace as this mighty king would humbly enter the city riding on the back of a donkey. This Messiah would come in peace to redeem "that which was lost." The image sends the message that the Kingdom of God will not come by force or threat; but will be built in the hearts of repentant people who choose Jesus as their servant king.

Thy kingdom come, thy will be done (Matthew 6:10).

PRAYER: Dear Jesus, You are our King. We rejoice greatly because you entered the world to pay the price for our salvation. For this, we praise your Holy Name. Lord, You came to us the first time in humility and in a lowly state. But we know that when You return

– You will come with splendor and power. May we live our lives in great expectation of your coming again.

[Zechariah 9:9 ESV]

Malachi

For I am the Lord, I change not; therefore ye sons of Jacob are not consumed (3:6 KJV). And they shall be mine, saith the Lord of hosts, in that day when I make up my jewels (3:17a)

The people of Israel had continued to struggle with their relationship with God. God could have completely destroyed the people and cited their refusal to obey. But God is faithful and loving and always keeps His Word. God never changes. God promised Abraham that he would multiply Abraham's seed until it was countless. This is why Abraham's descendants, the people who rebelled, were not totally destroyed. The Prophet Malachi reminded the people that God never changes – even though people change and turn from God. God always keeps His promise to redeem and to love Abraham's seed - not because *they* deserved it – but because God never changes.

The Lord even referred to His people as *jewels* which tells us that they were precious in God's sight. He said this though they were often rebellious. Jewels are precious and costly and, as a matter of fact, jewels reflect the light when held up against it.

The Lord is the light of the world - and in Him there is no darkness at all. There is no changing of the depth of His love – even when we do not deserve it. There is nothing that one can do to win more of His love and nothing to cause Him to love less. God's Son has already demonstrated the unparalleled depth of God's love. Amen

My friend, as you Facetime with God, I offer this prayer for you which was offered by the Apostle Paul in Ephesians 3:16-21:

PRAYER: *I pray that out of his glorious riches, he may strengthen you with power through his Spirit in your inner being, so that Christ may dwell in your hearts through faith. And I pray that you, being rooted and established in love, may have power, together with all the Lord's holy people, to grasp how wide and long and high and deep is the love of Christ, and to know this love that surpasses knowledge- that you may be filled to the measure of all the fulness of Now unto him who is able to do immeasurably more than all we ask or imagine, according to his power that is at work within us, to him be glory in the church and in Christ Jesus throughout all generations, for ever and ever! Amen.*

[Malachi 3:6, 17 KJV]

Matthew: What Do You Want?

And Jesus stood still, and called them and said, "What will ye that I shall do unto you?

Jesus was leaving Jericho and as usual a great crowd was following him. It happened that two blind men were sitting by the side of road as Jesus was passing their way. The men called out begging for facetime with the Lord. "Have mercy on us, O Lord, thou Son of David." How could they know that Jesus, heir to the throne of David, was indeed the Savior of the world and how could they know that he could heal their blinded eyes? Somehow, they knew that Jesus had the power, if only they could get his attention. The crowd tried to deter them. But Jesus stood still, heard their cries, and called to them asking: "w*hat do you want me to do for you?"*.

Can you believe that even today, Jesus still passes our way? And, if you call to him, you will find that you too can get his attention. The world with its busyness, noise and chaos will always turn you away. But Jesus will stand still and hear what you have to say.

Prayer: Good morning Lord. Thank you for another day. Thank you for the privilege of prayer. I worship you. I can also ask what I will, and you hear and will answer. You love to hear my voice. You do not scold but invite me into your Presence. I am happy to Facetime God.

[Matthew 20:32 KJV]

Mark: Who's in Your Corner?

When Jesus saw their faith, he said to the paralyzed man, Son, your sins are forgiven.

Have you ever been paralyzed such that you were not able to move without the help of others? Perhaps, you were gripped by fear, the doubt that you could achieve something or the very thought that your physical abilities did not match the task that lay before you. One day, I asked some children what the word *paralyze* meant to them. And, out of the mouth of babes, one child said that it means to be, "without strength".

In this story from Mark chapter 2, we learn that the friends of a man who was paralyzed had brought him to Jesus. This is a favorite miracle to me because it raises the question of *'who is in your corner when you cannot move forward on your own?'.* Who will carry you and where will they take you? If they are not bringing you closer to the Lord, perhaps you need friends who will. Are you such a friend to others? Do you bring your friends to Jesus? While we may not be able to physically bring people to church, we can always bring them face to face with God through prayer, personal testimony, and even through witnessing for what God has done.

A second important point in this text is Jesus' message about forgiveness. Do you know someone who is without strength, who needs forgiveness, or perhaps needs to forgive? Many times, the failure to forgive is what prevents us from *moving forward* and leaves us literally *without strength*. Ask God for forgiveness and learn to forgive others

Prayer: Dear Father, we *come boldly before Your throne of grace that we might obtain mercy and find grace to help us in this time of need.* We boldly ask for forgiveness, for healing, for restoration, for salvation and for refreshing. Help us to be reconciled to You and to one another. This pandemic has thrust us into a time of uncertainty. Help us to *believe*. And, help us to overcome our *unbelief*. Thank you for the invitation to facetime you boldly. Thank you for hearing and answering our prayers. In the name of Jesus, the living Christ. Amen. (Hebrews 4:16).

[Mark 2:5 NIV]

For with God, nothing shall be impossible. (The angel said this after making this announcement to Mary), *"behold, thou shalt conceive in thy womb and bring forth a son, and you are to call his name JESUS." vs 31.*

The immaculate conception of Jesus fulfilled many promises in this scripture including God's plan for the redemption of humanity, for salvation, healing, adoption and so much more. In addition, the covenant with the House of David was fulfilled that the throne of David would have no end. Jesus is the fulfillment of Davidic prophecy as the final king who lives and reigns forever. His birth through a virgin was indeed miraculous. But, his marvelous acts in death proved with finality that "with God, anything is possible." Satan thought that he had won in his efforts to kill Jesus. But he had not counted on the power of Almighty God to raise Jesus from the dead. He had not counted on God bestowing all power on His Son such that Jesus would claim victory over death, Hell, and condemnation. Therefore, humanity was not only saved, but no longer feared death as its enemy. God performed the ultimate miracle of sending his son to redeem humanity and to restore that which was lost back to himself. With God, nothing shall be impossible.

Because of Jesus, you and I are able to facetime God.

Dear God,

Thank you that we can have the confidence that Your power has no limits. There is absolutely nothing that is beyond

Your ability. You made this abundantly clear when you gave us Your Son to reconcile our debt to sin. Your Son gave his life so that we could live. You raised your Son to life again and that same power is available to bring us into fellowship with our heavenly Father. Now we can facetime God fearlessly. With God all things are possible.

[Luke 1:31, 37 KJV]

John

And the Word was made flesh and dwelt among us, (and we beheld his glory, the glory as of the only begotten of the Father) full of grace and truth.

Because God wanted a closer relationship with you and me, he sent his son into the world – taking the form of a human being so that we might know more about God. We owe God a debt of gratitude and praise for sending His son in the flesh. Humanity was able to see him, to touch him and to know him. We beheld him. We facetimed him. And, we found him to be *full of grace and truth*. How amazing it is that God would reach out in such a personal way.

Someone once said that, "Christians should never lose their ability to marvel." We marvel at the wonderful works that God performs. We marvel at the miracles that he brings about in our lives. And, we marvel even more as we consider who He is. Jesus is the Son of God who was from the beginning. Jesus is the Word that was made flesh and dwelled among us. And, Jesus is God with us, therefore, we are never alone.

It is an awesome privilege to be able to talk with a God who is with us in prayer. Amazingly, when we talk with Him, something happens within us. We are better. Our load is made lighter, our vision is made brighter, and our heart is stronger.

Prayer. *Dear God, as I facetime you today, I pray specifically for those affected with and by coronavirus (that would be each of us).*

I pray that you would heal and direct us. Forgive us for being negligent when it comes to taking care of ourselves and each other. Deliver us and get the glory. Make us better because we have spent time in Your presence. In the name of the One who is filled with glory and truth. Amen

[John 1:14 KJV]

Acts

Men of Galilee, why do you stand gazing into heaven? This Jesus, who was taken up from you into heaven, will come in the same way as you saw him go into heaven.

The Lord Jesus ascended into heaven as his disciples and two men in white robes stood watching. The two men may have been the Lord's heavenly escorts sent to be witnesses of this important event. But it appears that they also had another mission. *"Why do you stand gazing into heaven?"* Their words brought the disciples out of the shock and amazement of seeing Jesus physically rise into the air and disappear into the clouds. They also confirmed the blessed assurance that Jesus would keep his promise to one day return (Matthew 14). Knowing this, the disciples began to publish the Good News that Jesus had gone away, but one day, he would come again.

Sometimes, we too become sidetracked with meaningless activity, when we could be involved in the important work of sharing the Good News about Jesus; that he died on a cross for our sins and that he rose again. More importantly, we must share the news that Jesus has gone away to heaven as he said (Matt. 14), and one day, he will return. In the words of that old Negro spiritual from the 1940s, "Ain't-a-that Good News?".

[Acts 1:11 ESV].

Romans

For I am persuaded that neither death nor life, nor angels, nor principalities, nor powers, nor things present, nor things to come, nor height, nor depth, nor any other created thing, shall be able to separate us from the love of God which is in Christ Jesus our Lord.

In this time of turmoil and uncertainty, it is common for people to express feelings of anxiety and worry. Our world is experiencing unparalleled chaos and disorder which some people have not seen in their lifetimes. Human behavior and morality have spiraled out of control. Moral and ethical values that once governed our lives have faded – and many people have developed the attitude that they can live their lives any way that they choose. Even our climate is affected by human conduct and behavior. The result has been an increase in the temperature of the earth causing natural disasters such as hurricanes, earthquakes, wildfires and flooding. Violence and hatred are fueling anger and division among us as well as the loss of life. Many people may already view the year of 2020 as the most corrupt and violent that recent history has seen.

But, as troubling as the times have become, the people of God must never fear because God is still in control. I am persuaded that the love of God has not diminished. And, I am convinced that those who love God will remain in His eternal care. Therefore, no matter how fearful the world around us might become, *absolutely nothing - anything or anyone" (including death itself)* - can ever separate us from the eternal, everlasting,

and faithful love of God which is in Christ Jesus. It is a Promise
that you can stand on. Amen.
[Romans 8:38-39 NKJV]

I Corinthians

For we speak the wisdom of God in a mystery: even the hidden wisdom, which God ordained before the world unto our glory, which none of the princes of this world knew. For had they known it, they would not have crucified the Lord of glory. But, as it is written, eye hath not seen, nor ear heard, neither have entered into the heart of man, the things which God hath prepared for them that love him. But God hath revealed them to us by his Spirit ...

Yes! God's plan is awesome! His purpose magnificent! It is a mystery that has been revealed only to those who love Him. The Apostle Paul was sharing the divine truth that those who do not have the Spirit of God could not know the plan or God, and therefore, could not know the truth that Jesus, the son of God, came into the world to save sinners. Paul says that, if they had known, they would not have crucified him. But God sent his Spirit to reveal the truth to those who love him. By His Spirit, you and I are able to know the Truth which makes us free! This truth has been revealed, and yet, "the half has never been told." There is more to know.

This is the ultimate checkmate in chess, the hole-in-one, and the coup de grace over Satan's ability to hold God's people in condemnation. Clearly, what the enemy meant for evil, God has turned for our good - even for our redemption. Oh, the love of God! The Apostle Paul prayed that we would come to know the *depth, the breadth, and the height* of God's love. Do you want to know more? God desires facetime.

72

Prayer: *We worship you Lord. We praise and honor You - not just for what you have done —although we are still in awe, but for who You are – the Lord of Glory!*

[First Corinthians 2:7-10a; Ephesians 3:18 KJV].

II Corinthians

Blessed be the God and Father of our Lord Jesus Christ - the Father of compassion and the God of all comfort - who comforts us in all our troubles, so that we can comfort those in any trouble with the comfort we ourselves have received from God.

Many of us have felt the comfort of God when we have experienced the difficult and challenging times of sorrow and deep hurt. It was possibly a pain that only a compassionate and loving God could understand; a time when all that you could offer up were deep moans or groans of agony. God understands our feelings of sorrow and despair – pain that is too deep for words. This is why his mercies and tender compassions are new every morning. So that as we journey through the long, dark, and lonely times of sorrow, we can rest in the calm assurance that we are not alone; that the face of God is turned toward us.

Especially in times of loss and grief, God is there to dispatch his ambassadors to be at your side to help you to get through the tough parts of the journey. God gives you a sense of peace and a *life jacket* of love that keeps you from giving in to the pain or turning to thoughts of self-harm. God provides the anchor that keeps our soul afloat and your hope alive until such time as you can emerge stronger though you may still feel the pain. Healing begins to take the form of reaching out to others who are going through the sad journey that you have trod. God desires facetime with you as you extend the grace that you have received.

Prayer: *Compassionate Father, I pray for those who are grieving and can hardly articulate their sorrow and pain. We stand on the promise that You are with us always. You bottle up every tear and understand every groan. Surround us with your peace and may we feel your loving embrace. Thank you for sending someone who has a listening ear and a understanding heart that reflects your grace to walk with me through this journey.* Amen [*Second Corinthians 1:3-4 BSB]*

Galatians

Stand fast therefore in the liberty wherewith Christ has made us free. It is for freedom that Christ has set us free. Stand firm, then, and do not let yourselves be burdened again by a yoke of bondage [slavery]. But the fruit of the Spirit is love, joy, peace, longsuffering, gentleness, goodness, faith, meekness, and temperance.

Many followers of Christ are bound by made-man rules and traditions which some have mistakenly adopted as commandments of God. They have missed the lesson that God is more interested in our *being* than in our *doing.* This is because Jesus Christ has already done the work and through him, we have become the *righteousness of God.* We cannot do enough, look holy enough or talk pure enough to win more points toward our liberty or freedom from sin. Jesus has paid the price in full. This means that God does not need or want *legalistic* followers – those who think that they can do something to help to guarantee their salvation. In fact, if salvation could be achieved by what you do, it would put you in a place of duty, obligation, and burden which you could never achieve. Instead, Jesus has finished the work and God has given us freedom through Jesus and his Spirit which produces fruit that is light.

We are free because our Lord has paid the full account for our sin. So, let us not return to the weights and the sins that so easily beset us. Which fruit are you exhibiting today?

[Galatians 5:1, 22 KJV, NIV]

Ephesians

But now in Christ Jesus, ye who sometimes were far off are made nigh (near) by the blood of Christ. For he is our peace, who hath made both one, and hath broken down the middle wall of partition between us… For through him (Christ) we both have access by one Spirit unto the Father.

The **ultimate** reason that we are able to "FaceTime God" is because through his Son, the partition that had once kept us apart has been destroyed. When Jesus gave his life on the cross and paid the debt of sin which humanity owed, the partition or barrier that separated us from God was forever torn away. It means that because of what Jesus has done, we now have open access to God. So, whether one is Jewish, Gentile, male or female, young or old, rich or poor, all have equal access to God. It does not matter where you live, where you come from or how you vote. Access is granted!

This my dear ones, is the good news of the Gospel. I repeat – all have full access to the Father through Jesus Christ. Why not take a moment to facetime God right now?

[Ephesians 2:13, 18 KJV].

Philippians

Being confident of this very thing, that he which hath begun a good work in you will perform it until the day of Jesus Christ ...

This is one of my favorite scriptures in the entire Bible because as I am having my facetime with God, I also have the assurance that God is working in me. Regardless of the state of my mind, my body or my spirit, the Creator of the Universe has given me a passion, dream and purpose and is right now performing that good work in me. I am not hopeless or helpless. By the very grace of God, I am able to accomplish the work that God has begun in me. And so are you!

Can't you envision God smiling at the work that He is doing through you? Oh yes! And "the peace of God which passes all understanding, will keep your heart and mind through Christ Jesus (4:6)."

[Philippians 1:6; 4:6 KJV]

Colossians

And above all these things put on charity, which is the bond of perfectness. And let the peace of God rule in your hearts... and whatever ye do, do it heartily, as to the Lord, and not unto men.

To facetime with God is to facetime with Love. For God is love. Those who follow Christ should always walk in love. We allow the peace of God to govern our hearts when we walk in love. Everything that comes our way may not be lovely, but we do not have to curse the day or allow ourselves to give in to what is negative.

Love covers a multitude of wrongs. If a situation is not lovely, allow your love for God and the peace of God to guide your heart which guides your feet and directs your responses. It reduces stress and calms your blood pressure. If God is guiding your heart when you carry out a particular task, then you will not be consumed with pleasing others or trying to seek their approval. The approval of God is the highest compliment.

One day I had on a pair of socks that had hearts on them. I told my friend, "'Today I am walking in love." Before I could walk in love, I facetimed God to help me to reflect His love to those who were lovely and to those who were incorrigible. Amazingly, I was able to keep my peace and to be content that I had done my best for the Lord who tremendously blessed my effort. Believe me, a little facetime with God will keep you healthy.

[Colossians 3:14-15a, 23 KJV]

I Thessalonians

For our gospel came not unto you in word only, but also in power, and in the Holy Ghost, and in much assurance.

This walk in Christ is not just *word walk*, but a *life walk* that is *lived-in and lived-out*.

Just as faith without works is dead and one works because he or she has faith; this gospel is not a dormant message that we simply believe. The gospel is infused and empowered by *God the Father, God the Son, and God the Holy Spirit*. Therefore, we can have great assurance that when we facetime with God, the same power that raised Jesus from the dead is alive and available to us. This means that the earth-quaking, darkness shattering, lightning flashing, thunder roaring, fear demolishing to smithereens and explosive power of the Godhead exists in the life of every believer! Yes, this same strengthening force and invigorating power lives in you and me. As the Apostle Paul said, our gospel came to us "not in word only, but also in power."

The pastor is not the only one who is privileged to have this power. When you accepted Jesus Christ as Savior, you and I received this power also. So, nourish it! Cherish it! And, cultivate it! For I am convinced that it will reproduce one hundred-fold in your life. Take a few moments to facetime with God and let Him confirm this to you.

[First Thessalonians 1:5 KJV]

II Thessalonians

"...be not soon shaken in mind or be troubled, neither by spirit nor by word, nor by letter as that the day of Christ is at hand."

The second letter that the Apostle Paul wrote to the church in Thessalonica was written during a time of great peril for Christians and many were convinced that the end of civilization had to be soon. This is why the Apostle Paul wrote to encourage them to stand firm in their faith and to rest assured that believers would be able to see the signs of Jesus's impending return. Sometimes, Christians today have the same worries as they marvel at the amount of violence and turmoil in the world and wonder whether Jesus is about to come back.

But, as we facetime with God, we are reminded that although we face trials and tribulations and even persecution, the time for Jesus' return has not yet come. The scriptures tell us that there must be signs of his coming: a great falling away from the church; the coming of an evil one whom people will worship as God; an evil one who will enter the church and speak – but will not speak the Truth. He will have no part in Jesus who is t*he way, the truth, and the life (John 14:6).*

Believers should not be amazed at the mounting sin and evil that they will witness as we all await the blessed return of the Savior. Our faith will be challenged as never before, and evil will confront us at every hand. So be prepared to stand firm, stand assured, and stand confidently convinced that the Great Day of His Coming will happen – soon.

PRAYER: *Now, the Lord of peace himself give you peace always by all means. The Lord be with you all (3:16).* The face of God is Peace; the face of God is Grace. Facetime with God gives you power and endurance to stand!

[Second Thessalonians 2:2 KJV]

I Timothy

*But godliness actually is a source of great gain when
accompanied by contentment (that contentment which comes
from a sense of inner confidence based on the sufficiency of God).*

Dear Lord, today I seek your face more so than your hand.
Many times, I am busy asking or seeking to attain things,
possessions, accolades, and prestige. When I pause to take an
assessment of what You have already provided, I come to the
reality that I do not need to reach for material goods. Rather, I
should seek to attain a life of godliness with contentment which
should more than suffice. You always supply all of my need and so
much more.

I thank you for the blessings of being in fellowship with
you through Christ Jesus. There is such a richness in being able to
bask in the light of your love. I am honored and tremendously
blessed to commune with You. I seek you with my whole heart,
my soul, and all of my strength. May my life always be a reflection
of You. Amen.

[First Timothy *6:6 AMP*]

II Timothy

For God hath not given us the spirit of fear; but of power, and of love, and of a sound mind.

As the Apostle Paul pens his second and last known letter to young Timothy before the time of Paul's execution, he instructs, encourages, and warns his pupil of the great responsibility that he must uphold. Perhaps, it was his way of committing Timothy and the work of the ministry into the hand of the Lord. Paul regards Timothy as a son whom he lovingly and confidently entrusts to the Lord. In some sense, he is calling on Timothy to "facetime" God as he urges him not to be afraid but to boldly face the challenges that lie ahead of him. Paul says, "therefore, endure hardness as a good soldier of Jesus Christ (2:3)."

Paul mentions Timothy's mother and grandmother (1:5). Many of us have also had parents or other family members to lead us to Christ through the conduct and behavior that they modeled before us. Their lives were testimonies to the faithfulness and grace of Jesus Christ which is a reminder that we too must persevere and do the same with our families. We should be models of Jesus showing his love, patience, mercy, and goodness.

Paul ends his letter by assuring Timothy that, "*I have fought a good fight, I have finished my course, I have kept the faith; (4:7-8, KJV).*

The Amplified Bible reads this way: *"I have fought the good and worthy and noble fight, I have finished the race, I have kept the faith [firmly guarding the gospel against error]. In the future there is reserved for me the [victor's] crown of righteousness [for being right with God and doing right], which the Lord, the righteous Judge, will award to me on that great day - and not to me only, but also to all those who have loved and longed for and welcomed His appearing. (AMP 4:7-8).*

Perhaps Paul is saying to Timothy, to you and to me **that it is** and **will all be worth it!**

[Second Timothy 1:7 KJV]

Titus

In hope of eternal life, which God, that cannot lie, promised before the world began... For the grace of God that brings salvation has appeared to all men...

God has made a promise which is unbreakable. He promised that "whosoever believeth in Him (Jesus) shall have eternal life." Therefore, God is a promise-maker and not a promise-breaker because he always keeps His promises. Someone even called him the *promise keeper* which seems fitting since God forever keeps His promises. Even before the foundation of the world and the beginning of time, God had formed His Plan for the salvation of humanity. This means that it will forever be true that "whosoever believes in Him shall have (the promise of) eternal life."

Thank you, Lord. In a world that highly regards the pedigree of certain people, their economic status and privilege, You offer the wonderful gift of salvation to anyone who believes. It does not matter who we are, what we possess or where we come from – You extend Your love to everyone. God, You speak every language. We do not have to wait until the 'sweet by and by' to receive Your Promise. We sit in heavenly places with Christ Jesus and have become joint heirs with him even now! I have the right and the privilege of calling God, Father. I have the right to facetime God. What a great joy. Woohoo!!

[Titus 1:2, 2:11 KJV]

Philemon

I always thank my God as I remember you in my prayers, because I hear about your love for all his holy people and your faith in the Lord Jesus.

What a beautiful vision of Christianity that is reflected in this text; the image of a body of faithful believers ever praying and being concerned about the struggles and problems of holy people everywhere. The Apostle Paul was touched by these faithful saints of God and he wanted them to know that he was likewise praying for them.

Facetime with God is a time that we can pray for others because God honors our prayers. In fact, one of the best ways to stop worrying about your own problems is to turn your attention in prayer to the concerns of others. This will take the spotlight off of ourselves. We can start by praying for our families, then move to pray for the body of Christ as these believers did back in Paul's day. We can then pray for the well-being of believers in our cities, states and across the nation. We can pray for others all around the world. And, do not forget to praise God for the faith and love of other believers.

Remember that just as we need to be relational with God, we must also be relational with the Saints of God throughout the world. We are all part of His Kingdom and our own faith is sharpened and encouraged when we hear about the experiences of others. Faith comes by hearing.

[Philemon 1:4-5 NIV]

Hebrews

Do not forget to show hospitality to strangers, for by so doing some people have shown hospitality to angels without knowing it.

With the world in such flux today, you can hardly find persons who will look around and speak to strangers passing by. Many persons are afraid to engage others in conversation for the fear of being misunderstood for having some type of underlying selfish motive, or afraid of being mugged. People are often afraid to speak with others because of apparent differences. What happens when those differences are not so apparent?

God calls us to be kind and hospitable to others. The story of the Good Samaritan demonstrates how a stranger was kind to someone who was hurt and left for dead by the side of the road. It was apparent that this man was hurt and in need. Today, we have opportunities to minister to others through kindness, respect, deeds, and sometimes through engaging others in conversations. Others may or may not look like you on the outside but are hurting or wounded on the inside.

We may meet a stranger at work, at school or in our own places of worship.

God is pleased when we are selfless and concerned about others. The very instance that you are welcoming and gracious to others may be the very moment that you are welcoming and gracious to the very face of God. We are all made in the image of God.

Now the God of Peace makes you perfect in every good work to do His will; working in you that which is well pleasing in His sight through Jesus Christ (13:20).

James

Faith without works [deeds] is useless.

James reminds us that our faith will be put to the test and it will only be backed up by the work that we do. *Faith without works is dead.* We must do more than just believe that Jesus is the Son of God who died for the sins of the world. Our faith in Jesus ought to be reflected in the deeds that we perform especially in difficult times. James tells us that demons *believe* and tremble. Therefore, we ought to do more to display who we are as followers of Christ. James is saying that it is easy to have faith when everything is going well. But, will we be able to display the strong muscles of faith when times get hard? Flabby faith results from words and no action. The testing of our faith creates strength to persevere. Happy and blessed is the one whose faith continues to stand when it is challenged and tested.

James tells us that we must be participators of the Word of God and not just someone who merely listens. Have you ever received a credit card that had to be activated? Basically, the card is a dud until you take action that will empower it for use. Let's activate our faith so that we are believers with power.

[James 2:20 NIV].

I Peter

For the eyes of the Lord are over the righteous and his ears are attentive to their prayer, but the face of the Lord is against those who do evil.

The Lord watches over everyone who obeys Him, and God's vision is more than a mere observation. The writer of Second Chronicles puts it this way: *The eyes of the Lord run throughout the whole earth to show himself strong on the behalf of them whose heart is perfect toward Him (II Chron 16:9).*

Of course, we know that God is also a Spirit and that He does not have the form of a man which means, that He does not need bodily features such as eyes, hands or a heart. But the writer gives us these anthropomorphic images so that we may better understand the immeasurable breadth of God's strength and power. God's vision is like God's plan. It is good for mankind because when we understand that God sees everything, this knowledge ought to cause us to feel closer to God. If we can envision the image of God's *seeing* and therefore *knowing* everything that happens in the world, then we can be assured that nothing is beyond the knowledge or understanding of God. The songwriter said, "He's got the whole world in His hands."

So, God is always aware of us. We can facetime God, but actually God facetimes us. God has a vision for every life. Exhale and rest in knowing that God sees you. God knows you. And, God hears every beat of your heart. Wow! What a Mighty God we serve!

[First Peter 3:12]

II Peter

Moreover, I will be careful to ensure that you always have a reminder of these things after my decease (death).

Can you imagine elderly parents sharing words of wisdom and encouragement with the children that they are leaving behind? Realizing that they will not live forever, the parents want to ensure that their children are ready to carry on after they are gone. The Apostle Peter is sharing a similar message with believers as he prepares them to keep their faith in Jesus Christ even after he is done.

Peter writes to encourage his friends as he knew his death was imminent. This is a different type of facetime which may be intercessory whereby we bring our thoughts and concerns about others into facetime with God. Peter wanted these believers to build their faith by adding a litany of spiritual virtues that would make them stronger and enable them to become mature and well-grounded in their faith. Peter said, "If these qualities are yours and are increasing, they keep you from being ineffective or unfruitful…" (v.8). He assured them that God would provide everything that they need even after he is done.

It is important for every believer to realize that we will not live forever. Therefore, we should consider imparting words of wisdom and encouragement to our children, family, and friends to "keep the faith" in Jesus Christ after we are gone.

[Second Peter 1:15]

I John

See what great love the Father has lavished on us that we should be called children of God! (3:1). Dear friends, let us love one another for love is of God (4:7) ... we love him, because he first loved us (4:19). And this is the record, that God has given to us eternal life, and this life is in his Son (5:11).

One of the most compelling points that is made by the writer of First John is that if one is truly a follower of Jesus Christ, then he or she must have love for God and for others. John, the disciple whom Jesus loved, said we love him because he loved us first. Then, he invites the reader to consider the great love that God has lavished upon us. The word "lavished" is written in the past tense which lets us know that this is action that has already been taken. The Father has already poured out his love upon us. According to standard literary sources, "to lavish" means to bestow in generous or extravagant quantities or to cover excessively (Dictionary.com). The Father has generously poured out his love which cannot be contained. It is love that is out-of-the-box, overflowing, over-reaching, and liberally flowing in our lives. See what great love the Father has for us?

In his letter to the Romans, the Apostle Paul said it this way... "God commended his love toward us in that while we were yet sinners, Christ died for us". This means that God's overarching love was extended toward us even before we said, "Yes, we will follow you." As a matter of fact – it still reaches to the highest heights and flows to the lowest low. It reaches out to cover you and me no matter who you are or where you are in the world or in life. So, now might be a good time to Facetime with a Loving God – regardless of where you live or where you come from - and say, 'thank you, much obliged, gracias, merci beaucoup, danke, grazie, arigato, mahalo, toda' or thank you in any language.

[First John 3:1, 4:7,19; 5:11 NIV]

II John

"It has given me great joy to find some of your children walking in the truth, just as the Father commanded us" (vs 4).

Second John is a brief letter which was written to make a single point to the church. The writer is filled with joy that believers and the offspring of believers are holding fast to the truth of God's Word and are walking in the ways of the Lord. No greater joy can come to any pastor or spiritual leader than to know that members of his or her congregation are embracing the gospel and walking in truth. Facetime with God.

Dear Lord, at this time, we pray that our children receive and accept Jesus Christ as Lord and Savior of their lives. We pray that they will be able to discern the truth of God's love which came through His Son from other voices that are competing presently in the world. We pray that our children will also become witnesses to their peers through their walk. We thank you that our children are walking in Your truth and in Your love. In Christ name, Amen

II John 1:4 NIV]

95

III John

"Beloved, I pray that you may prosper in all things and be in health, just as your soul prospers. (vs 1: 2). Or Dear friend, do not imitate what is evil, but what is good (vs. 1:11).

The beloved John wrote this letter to encourage believers to remain true to the gospel and to follow the ways of Christ which they have been taught. He prayed for their health and strength of body, mind, and spirit as he echoed warnings from previous writings to beware of false teachers and of people who will attempt to lead them from the ways that they have been taught.

God is concerned with our physical health. We cannot take health for granted. There is also a need for balance in diet, exercise, and rest. The body and the mind need to be nourished as well as the spirit. We need to be mindful to receive the same grace that we extend to others when we encourage self-care and self-love.

Some individuals within the church were refusing to show hospitality and love to visitors and strangers because they were not affiliated with that church. But John said that the church ought to help those who are spreading the gospel no matter where they come from. Believers must always be willing to show their love to others. This is a lesson to the church of today that believers ought to be supportive of efforts to carry the word of Truth into the world – no matter which church might be doing it.

Beloved, do not imitate what is evil but imitate what is good. Whoever does good is from God; whoever does evil has not seen God (v.13).

[III John 1:2, 11, 13 NKJV}

Jude

Jude, a servant of Jesus Christ and brother of James, to those who are called, who are beloved in God the Father and kept safe for Jesus Christ: May mercy, peace, and love be yours in abundance (v.1-2).

Jude, the brother of Jesus had become a prominent leader in the church and, like the Apostle Paul, was gravely concerned about maintaining the purity of the gospel. He warned believers to watch out for those who would attempt to pervert the message of Jesus Christ in ways that would allow them to engage in all types of immoral behavior. These were people who claimed to have spiritual authority that was above that of other believers. And so, they claimed that they did not need to submit to the authority of the church. Jude told believers that they must remember the earlier warnings that the disciples had given that, "In the last times, there will be scoffers indulging their own ungodly lusts."

This is a warning and a reminder to believers everywhere today that some will come into the church and attempt to water-down the message of the gospel so that it will suit their own permissive lifestyle. But those who are "called and beloved of God the Father" should know and stand on the truth and not allow this to happen. Jude gives this resolute closing to his letter:

Now to him who is able to keep you from stumbling and to present you blameless before the presence of his glory with great joy, to the only God, our Savior, through Jesus Christ our Lord, be glory, majesty, dominion, and authority, before all time - now and forever more. Amen.

Facetime with the One who is well-able to keep you and to present you – and me – to Our Heavenly Father with great joy!

[Jude 1:1-2, 24-25]

Revelation

He who was seated on the throne said, I am making everything new! Then He said, Write this down, for these words are trustworthy and true. He said to me: It is done. I am Alpha and the Omega, the Beginning and the End. To the thirsty, I will give water without cost from the spring of the water of life (21:5-6).

God wants to do a new thing in our lives. Not just in the *sweet by and by*, but God wants to do a new thing in our lives right now. Are you thirsty for something new and amazing that will change your life forever? I want to assure you that your thirst can be quenched through a fulfilling and satisfying relationship with Jesus Christ. Often, we try to fill our thirsty void with objects of pleasure, with people or with something that we can buy. But it only results in temporary relief and the end result is that we are thirstier than before.

God has living water that will satisfy and quench the thirstiest thirst. The One who sits on the throne has the true and living water and it is free to those who ask him for it. It is a gift of great value. The living water will motivate and energize you to live a life that is well-pleasing to God. God has promised to freely give this living water to all who would ask. Are you thirsty for the Living Water? Facetime God.

[Revelation 21:5-6 NIV]